INTERMITTENT
FASTING

Diet Cookbook to Boost Your
Metabolism and Accelerate
Weight Loss

Carola Taylor

TABLE OF CONTENTS

Introduction 1

What Is Intermittent...3

The Science Behind It 4

Health Benefits of Intermittent Fasting.....................6

    Activating Cellular Repair.....................................7

    Increase Cognitive Function and Protects the Brain 7

    Weight Loss 7

    Alleviates Oxidative Stress and Inflammation 8

    Slow Down the Aging Process 8

    Ultimate Steps for Getting Started 8

    A Step-by-Step Approach 10

Breakfast for Your Intermittent Fast 13

    Banana Orange Smoothie 14

    Crunchy Banana Yoghurt......................................15

    Carrot Breakfast Salad 15

    Delicious Turkey Wrap 17

    Cherry Smoothie Bowl 18

    Sausage Quiche with Tomatoes..............................20

    Fitness Burger With Omelet and Salmon 21

    Eggs and Salsa...22

    Delicious Shakshuka 24

    Homemade Tuna Fish Cakes & Lemon Sauce 26

Lunch 28

    Pasta Bolognese 29

Eggs with chilli and red Beans............30

Pork Carnitas............32

Turkey Walnut Salad............33

Parmesan Chicken with Zucchini............35

Grilled Shrimp Easy Seasoning............37

The Best Garlic Cilantro Salmon............38

Cauliflower Crust Pizza............40

Aromatic Dover Sole Fillets............42

Falafel and Tahini Sauce............44

Dinner............46

Spring Ramen Bowl............47

Freekeh Salad............48

Garlic Shrimp with Zucchini Noodles............50

Veggie-stuffed Omelet............52

Picadillo Chicken............53

Instant Pot Teriyaki Chicken............55

Mixed Vegetables and Chicken Egg Rolls............56

Cauliflower Mashed Potatoes............59

Sheet Pan Steak Fajitas............60

Coated Cauliflower Head............63

Snacks for Tasting............65

Roasted Brussels sprouts With Mushrooms............66

Eggplant Fries............67

Parmesan Crisps............69

Roasted Broccoli............70

Healthy Salmon Sandwich............71

Santorini Bay Salad 72

Baked Fennel 74

Summer Swiss Chard 75

Tofu and Broccoli Salad...76

Desserts 79

Soles Banana Cupcakes..80

Almond Rice Dessert...81

Mango Cream..82

Chocolate Mousse 83

Berries with Ricotta Cream 84

Easy Chocolate Pudding..86

Almond Bites..87

Coconut Macaroon Cookies 89

Coconut Protein Balls 90

Vegan Coconut Kefir Banana Muffins....................................92

Conclusion 94

Introduction

Is it right for me?

I know intermittent fasting is very popular, or so they say. I know it's a quick and effective way to change my life and start seeing results in the shortest time possible.

I can guarantee that once you get used to eating on a schedule, it will soon feel like an effortless lifestyle change.

But how do you know if it's right for you? You will need to ask yourself a few questions to verify that you are in the right place before starting:

1. What is your motivation for fasting? Is it strong enough to keep you focused and carry on?

2. What do you want to achieve by fasting?

Do you have any health problems that could interfere? Should You Consult Your Doctor First?

4. Are there any obstacles that could emerge and take you off course during the first few weeks?

If so, this may prevent you from forming the fasting habit that will carry you forward.

But to keep it simple and to encourage you, I will try to simplify;

- Intermittent fasting is the process of abstaining from food and drink for a specific time.
- Intermittent fasting involves a cycle of feeding and fasting.
- Intermittent fasting does not so much determine what you should eat - but more about when you should eat.

There are many different ways you can take part in this fast - there is nothing set in stone, which means you can adapt it to your lifestyle no matter what.

Trust me, it's easy, and it's efficient!

What is Intermittent Fasting

During intermittent fasting, you would not be pressured to deprive yourself throughout the day, also mentioned as IF. It also doesn't grant you a license during the period of non-fasting to eat loads of unhealthy food. You consume within a fixed window of time, instead of consuming meals and treats all day. Intermittent fasting is an eating pattern model that requires daily, short-term fasts or limited or no food intake at times.

Most individuals know intermittent fasting as losing weight assistance. Intermittent fasting is a lifestyle that allows people to consume fewer calories, leading to weight loss over time.

Without being on an insane diet or consuming the calories to nil, it's a perfect way to get healthy.

Most of the time, when one begins intermittent fasting, they'll aim to maintain their calories the same as during a shortened time; most people consume larger meals. In comparison, prolonged fasting is a healthy way to preserve body mass while becoming lean. But most notably, intermittent fasting is among the most beneficial way to be in shape with many other benefits. This is an easy way to get the desired results. If performed properly, intermittent fasting will have valuable advantages, like weight reduction, type 2 diabetes reversal, and several other aspects. Plus, this will save time and resources for you.

Intermittent fasting is successful because it makes it possible for the amount of insulin and blood sugar to reach a low level. The body's fat-storing enzyme is insulin. Fat moves into the fat cells and gets absorbed when insulin levels are high in the blood; if insulin level is low, fat will move and burn out of fat cells. In short, IF is when food is readily available, but you prefer not to consume it. This may be over any period of time, from several hours to a couple of days, or sometimes a week or more under strict medical monitoring. You can begin fasting at any moment of your choice, and you can end a fast at your will, too.

You fast intermittently if you don't consume food by choice. For instance, between dinner and breakfast, till the following day, you will not eat and fast for around 12 to 14 hours. Intermittent fasting can, in that way, be deemed a part of daily life.

The Science Behind it

Like any idea of eating that quickly takes over health and diet cultures, intermittent fasting has been suspected to be a fad. Still, the evidence behind fasting's advantages is already clear— and increasing.

There are several hypotheses as to why intermittent fasting performs so well, but tension has to do with the most widely studied — and most proven gain.

The term stress has been vilified continuously, but the body profits from some stress. Exercise, for example, is technically stress on the body (especially on the muscles and the cardiovascular system). Still, this specific stress ultimately makes the body better as long as you implement the correct amount of recovery period into your exercise plan.

Intermittent fasting stresses the body in the same way that exercise does; it brings the cells under moderate tension as you refuse the body food for a certain period. Cells respond to this tension over time by studying how to better cope with it. It has an improved ability to resist illness because the body becomes better at dealing with pain.

Health Benefits of Intermittent Fasting

When women get to 50 and over, their skin will start to show signs of age. They may find their joints start to ache for no reason, and suddenly belly fat accumulates as if you have just given birth. There are so many creams, diets and exercises on the market to tighten the skin and try to help. The fact is, they may work to a certain point but then the body hits a shelf, and nothing seems to push a person past it.

This boils up frustration making women look into the more drastic and very expensive alternatives like surgery.

Which in itself poses so many more dangers and risks for women of 50 and over.

A person does not need to go under the knife or starve themselves to reboot their system or change their shape. Intermittent fasting is a much cheaper and less risky way to do this and there is no need to make any drastic eating habits changes either. Well, you may need to make a few adjustments like cutting out junk food and eating healthier. But once again the diet a person follows is their personal choice and depends on how serious they are about becoming healthier.

Some health benefits of intermittent fasting
for women over 50 include:

Activating Cellular Repair

Fasting has been known to kick start the body's natural cellular repair function, get rid of mature cells, improve longevity, and improve hormone function. All things that tend to take a battering as people age. This can alleviate joint and muscle aches as well as lower back pain. As the cells are being repaired and the damage is undone, it helps with the skin's elasticity and health too.

Increase Cognitive Function and Protects the Brain

Intermittent fasting may increase the levels of a brain hormone known as a brain-derived neurotrophic factor (BDNF). It may equally guard the brain against damage like a stroke or Alzheimer's disease as it promotes new nerve cell growth. It also increases cognitive function and could effectively defend a person against other neurodegenerative diseases as well.

Weight Loss

When people have belly fat, it can cause many health problems that are associated with various diseases as it indicates a person has visceral fat. Visceral fat is fat that goes deep into the abdominal surrounding the organs. Belly fat is terribly hard to lose, especially for an aging woman. Intermittent fasting has been known to help reduce not only weight but inches of over five percent of body fat in around twenty-two to twenty-five weeks (Barna, 2019).

Alleviates Oxidative Stress and Inflammation

Oxidative stress is when the body has an imbalance of antioxidants as well as free radicals. This imbalance can cause both tissue and cell damage in overweight as well as aging people. It can also lead to various chronic illnesses like cancer, heart disease, diabetes, and also has an impact on the signs of aging. Oxidative stress can trigger the inflammation that causes these diseases.

Intermittent fasting can provide your system with a reboot, helping to alleviate oxidative stress and inflammation in a middle-aged woman. It also significantly reduces the risk of oxidative stress and inflammation for those overweight or obese.

Slow Down the Aging Process

As intermittent fasting gives both the metabolism and cellular repair a reboot it offers the potential to slow down aging. It may even prolong a person's lifespan by quite a few years especially if following a nutritious diet and exercise regime alongside intermittent fasting.

Ultimate Steps for Getting Started

Although intermittent fasting is a very simple and straightforward approach yet, fasting can be an intimidating word for many. Our dependence on food for our physical, mental, and emotional satisfaction has increased to such an extent that even the thought of abstinence from food can make people anxious. This is even more important in the case of women as controlling hunger for them can be very difficult. Their mind is internally programmed to look for food consciously.

This is a reason that although intermittent fasting is very easy and simple, some people may find it difficult to follow it in the long run.

The main reason some people may find intermittent fasting difficult to follow is not due to the severity of hunger or their inability to manage their routine but because they have not followed proper procedures.

Yes, you have read it right! The biggest reason people are unable to follow intermittent fasting is that they don't follow the process properly. They are so enthusiastic about losing weight that they don't give time to their bodies to prepare for the fasting schedules.

You must understand that humans have also evolved from animal species. Our first and foremost instinct is and always would be to eat, sleep, and procreate. If any hindrance is put in the way of either of these things, the initial reaction of our body would be adverse. If you try to snatch away any of these things or enforce stricter rules in these areas, the results are not going to be favorables.

No matter how beneficial fasting is for the body, the body is not going to react well to it initially. You will face the hunger pangs, cramps, distraction, mind wandering around food, irritability, and mood swings. There are ways to manage all these symptoms, but there can be no denying the fact that these issues will arise.

You can lower these adverse reactions by following proper protocols, and intermittent fasting will become a life-changing experience for you. If you jump the steps and rush to the last part in the first leg, you are bound to have severe symptoms, and not only the results would get affected, but you will also face problems in managing the lifestyle for long.

A Step-by-Step Approach

The best way to approach intermittent fasting is to move step by step. You must never undermine the fact that our lifestyles are heavily centered on food. There are shorter gaps between meals. There is a high amount of carb-intake that also aggravates the situation to a great extent.

If you follow a very hard approach from the word GO, you are bound to face adjustment issues. The best approach is to allow the body to adapt to the fasting schedule and let it build the capacity to stay hungry.

Eliminate Snacks

This is something that would come several times in this book. It is a very important thing that you must understand. The root cause of most of our health issues is the habit of frequent snacking.

Snacking leads to 2 major issues:

    1.It keeps causing repeated glucose spikes that invoke an insulin response and hence the overall insulin presence in the bloodstream increases aggravating the problem of insulin resistance.

    2.It usually involves refined carb and sugar-rich food items that will lead to cravings and you will keep feeling the urge to eat at even shorter intervals.

This is a reason your preparation for intermittent fasting must begin with the elimination of snacks. You can have 2-3 nutrient-dense meals in a day, but you will have to remove the habit of snacking from your routine.

As long as the habit of snacking is there, you'll have a very hard time staying away from food as this habit never allows your ghrelin response clock to get set at fixed intervals. This means that you will keep having urges to eat sweets and carb-rich foods, and you will also have strong hunger pangs at regular intervals.

The solution to this problem is very simple. You can take 2-3 nutrient-dense meals that are rich in fat, protein, and fiber. Such a meal will not only provide you with adequate energy for the day but would also keep your gut engaged for long so that you don't have frequent hunger pangs.

The farther you can stay away from refined carb-rich and sugar-rich food items, the easier you would find it to deal with hunger.

You must start easy. Don't do anything drastic or earth - shattering.

Simply start by lowering the number of snacks you have in a day. The snacks have not only become a need of the body, but they are also a part of the habit. In a day, there are numerous instances when we eat tit-bits that we don't care about. We sip cold-drinks, sweetened beverages, chips, cookies, bagels, donuts, burgers, pizzas simply because they are in front of us or accessible. We have made food an excuse to take breaks. This habit will have to be broken if you want to move on the path of good health.

Widen the Gap between Your Meals

This is the second step in your preparation. You must start widening the gap between your meals. This process needs to be gradual and should only begin when you have eliminated snacks from your routine. Two nutrient-dense meals in a day or two meals and a smaller meal or lunch comprising of fiber-rich salads should be your goal.

However, you must remember that these two steps must be taken over a long period. You must allow your body to get used to the change. There would be a temptation that it is easy to follow these, and you can jump to the actual intermittent fasting routine, but it is very important to avoid all such temptations as they are only going to lead to failures.

If your body doesn't get used to this routine, very soon, you'll start feeling trapped. You'll start finding ways to cheat the routine. You'll look for excuses to violate the routine, and it very soon becomes a habit. This is the reason you must allow your body to take some time to adjust to the new schedule.

You should remember that intermittent fasting is a way of life. This might slower the results, but it is going to make your overall journey smoother and better.

Breakfast for Your Intermittent Fast

Banana Orange Smoothie

Preparation time: 10 minutes

Cooking time: 0 minutes

Servings: 2

Nutrition:

- calories 183,
- fat 8g,
- fiber 1g,
- carbs 3g,
- protein 9g

Ingredients:

2 cups fat free milk

1 cup nonfat Greek yogurt

1 medium banana

1 cup collard greens

1 orange, peeled, deseeded, separated into segments

6 strawberries, chopped

2 tbsp. sesame seeds

Direction:

1.Add all the ingredients in a blender and blend until smooth.

2.Pour in glasses and serve.

Crunchy Banana Yoghurt

Preparation time: 10 min

Cooking time: 0 minutes

Servings: 4

Nutrition:

- calories 323,
- fat 11g,
- fiber 4g,
- carbs 13g,
- protein 17g

Ingredients:

3 cups fat free natural Greek style yogurt

1 ounce mixed seeds or nuts of your choice like
   pumpkin seeds etc.

2 bananas, sliced

Direction:

1. Take 4 bowls and add ¾ cup yogurt into each bowl.
2. Divide the banana slices among the bowl.
3. Sprinkle seeds on top and serve.

Carrot Breakfast Salad

Preparation Time: 5 minutes

Cooking Time: 4 hours

Servings: 4

Nutrition:

- Calories: 437,
- Protein: 2.39 grams,

- Fat: 39.14 grams
- Carbs: 23.28 grams

Ingredients:

- 2 tablespoons olive oil
- 2 pounds' baby carrots, peeled and halved
- 3 garlic cloves, minced
- 3 celery stalks, chopped
- 2 yellow onions, chopped
- ½ cup vegetable stock
- 1/3 cup tomatoes, crushed
- A pinch of salt and black pepper

Directions:

1. In your slow cooker, combine all the ingredients, cover and cook on high for 4 hours.
2. Divide into bowls and serve for breakfast.

Delicious Turkey Wrap

Preparation Time: 10 minutes

Cooking Time: 10 minutes

Servings: 6

Nutrition:

- Calories: 162,
- Fat: 4 g
- Carbohydrates: 7 g
- Protein: 23 g

Ingredients:

- 1 and a ¼ pounds of ground turkey, lean
- 4 green onions, minced
- 1 tablespoon of olive oil
- 1 garlic clove, minced
- 2 teaspoons of chili paste
- 8 ounces water chestnut, diced
- 3 tablespoons of hoisin sauce

- 2 tablespoons of coconut amino
- 1 tablespoon of rice vinegar
- 12 butter lettuce leaves
- 1/8 teaspoon of salt

Directions:

1. Take a pan and place it over medium heat, add turkey and garlic to the pan

2. Heat for 6 minutes until cooked

3. Take a bowl and transfer turkey to the bowl

4. Add onions and water chestnuts

5. Stir in hoisin sauce, coconut amino, vinegar, and chili paste

6. Toss well and transfer the mix to lettuce leaves. Serve and enjoy.

Cherry Smoothie Bowl

Preparation Time: 15 minutes

Cooking Time: 0 minute

Servings: 1

Nutrition:

- Calories: 130,
- Carbs: 32 g
- Fat: 5g
- Protein: 1 g

Ingredients:

(Soak the organic rolled oats in half a cup of unsweetened almond milk)

- ½ cup of organic rolled oats

- ½ cup almond milk-unsweetened
- 1 tablespoon Chia seeds
- 2 teaspoons granola
- 2 teaspoons almonds sliced
- 1 tablespoon almond butter
- 1 teaspoon vanilla extract
- ½ cup berries-fresh
- 1 cup Cherries- Frozen
- 1 cup plain Greek yogurt

Directions:

1. Prepare a smooth blend of soaked oats, frozen cherries, yogurt, chia seeds, almond butter, and vanilla extract. Pour the mixture into two bowls.

2. In each bowl, add equal parts of hemp seeds, sliced almonds, and fresh berries.

Sausage Quiche with Tomatoes

Preparation Time: 15 minutes

Cooking Time: 10 minutes

Servings: 6

Nutrition:

- Cal 340;
- Net Carbs 3g;
- Fat 28g;
- Protein 1.7g

Ingredients:

6 eggs

12 oz. raw sausage rolls

10 cherry tomatoes, halved

2 tbsp. heavy cream

2 tbsp. Parmesan, grated

Salt and black pepper to taste

2 tbsp. parsley, chopped

5 eggplant slices

Directions:

1. Preheat the oven to 370 F. Chop the sausage rolls into the bottom of a greased pan and the eggplant slices on top of the sausage.

2. Bake for 10 minutes, then leave to rest for a few minutes.

3. Complete with the cherry tomatoes. Beat the eggs together with the cream, Parmesan, salt, and pepper.

4. Pour the egg mixture over the sausage. Bake for about 20 minutes. Serve sprinkled with parsley.

Fitness Burger With Omelet and Salmon

Preparation Time: 10 minutes

Cooking Time: 6 minutes

Servings: 2

Nutrition:

- Cal 514;
- Net Carbs 5.8g;
- Fat 47g;
- Protein 37g

Ingredients:

1 cup rocket

2 loaves of wholemeal flour

2 tbsp. chopped chives

2 oz. smoked salmon, sliced

1 spring onion, sliced

4 eggs, beaten

3 tbsp. cream cheese

1 teaspoon linseed oil

Salt and black pepper to taste

Directions:

1. In a small bowl, combine the chives and cream cheese; set aside. Season the eggs with salt and pepper. Melt butter in a pan and add the eggs; cook for 3 minutes.

2. Flip the omelet over and cook for another 2 minutes until golden.

3. Place them on the bread and spread the chive mixture. Complete with salmon and onion slices. Cover with another slice of bread and serve.

Eggs and Salsa

Preparation time: 5 minutes

Cooking time: 5 minutes

Servings: 4

Nutrition:

- calories 340,
- fat 14g,
- fiber 4g,
- carbs 3g,

- protein 5g,

Ingredients:

- 1 red pepper, chopped
- 1 cups tomatoes sauce
- 1 green onion (bunch)
- 1 bunch cilantro, chopped
- 1 cup red onion, chopped
- Juice from 1 lime
- 2 small habanero chilies, chopped
- 2 garlic cloves, minced
- 4 eggs, whisked
- A drizzle of olive oil
- Sea salt

Directions:

1. Mix the tomatoes, green onions, red onion, habanero, garlic, cilantro, lime juice, and mix well.

2. Heat a pan with a drizzle of oil, add the eggs and mix for 2 minutes

3. Add a pinch of salt and pour the mixture of tomato and vegetables.

4. Cook for another 5min.

5. Divide and serve on plates, add fresh cilantro and serve.

Delicious Shakshuka

Preparation time: 10 minutes

Cooking time: 30 minutes

Servings: 4

Nutrition:

- calories 40,
- fat 1g,
- fiber 2g,
- carbs 8g,
- protein 2g

Ingredients

Feta cheese crumbled half a cup

Eggplant cut into cubes, half a cup

Sliced courgette, half a cup

Two tablespoons extra virgin olive oil.

Four eggs

One sliced onion

Black pepper powder one teaspoon.

Sliced red sweet peppers

A quarter of a teaspoon of salt.

Three minced garlic cloves

Red pepper flakes half a teaspoon.

Three pureed tomatoes

Coriander half a teaspoon.

Ground cumin two tsp.

Paprika a teaspoon.

Fresh chopped parsley a teaspoon.

Pieces of almond bread

Directions

1. Preheat the oven to 375 ° C.

2. Heat the olive oil in a large skillet over medium heat.

3. Add the sliced onion and let it fry until it has a nice golden color. Complete with the pieces of red pepper, aubergine, zucchini, and cook until the peppers are soft.

4. Also, add the minced garlic cloves to this mixture and cook until the garlic is nice and fragrant.

5. Add the sliced tomato, cumin powder, coriander, paprika, and red pepper flakes. Also, add the salt and black pepper powder. Let this mixture cook for ten minutes until it thickens.

6. Take a large pan and pour in the cooked sauce. With a spoon, make eight holes in the sauce and each slot an egg and pour it.

7. Sprinkle some salt and pepper on the eggs for seasoning. Using aluminum foil, cover the pan and transfer it to the oven that you previously heated for a quarter of an hour until the eggs are well cooked.

8. When they are ready, sprinkle the crumbled feta with fresh parsley.

9. Cut into slices and serve with the almond bread.

Homemade Tuna Fish Cakes & Lemon Sauce

Preparation time: 10 minutes

Cooking time: 20 minutes

Servings: 1

Nutrition:

- calories 350,
- fat 8g,
- fiber 2g,
- carbs 8g,
- protein 26g

Ingredients

For the tuna cakes:

- Half a zucchini, grated
- 1 can of drained tuna
- 2 tbsp oats

- 2 tbsp cheese, shredded
- 1 egg
- 0.24 tsp garlic salt
- 0.25 tsp dill
- 0.25 tsp onion powder

For the sauce:
- 2 tbsp yogurt, Greek-style is best
- 1 tsp juice of a lemon
- 0.25 tsp dill
- 0.25 tsp garlic salt

Direction

1. Take a piece of cheesecloth, or similar and place the grated zucchini inside, twisting so that all the liquid comes out
2. In a medium bowl, place the drained zucchini inside and add the tuna, oats, shredded cheese, the garlic salt, dill, onion powder, pepper, and the egg, combining everything together well
3. Take a large frying pan and add a little olive oil, or cooking spray if you prefer
4. Take half of the mixture and form a ball, before flattening it into a fish cake style, repeating with the other half
5. Place the cakes into the frying pan, cooking over medium heat for around 6 minutes on each side
6. Meanwhile, combine the sauce ingredients into a small mixing bowl and ensure they are mixed together well
7. Once the fish cakes are cooked place them on a serving plate and allow to cool just slightly
8. Add a spoonful of the sauce on top and enjoy!

Lunch

Pasta Bolognese

Preparation time: 10 minutes

Cooking time: 35 minutes

Servings: 5

Nutrition:

- calories 182,
- fat 4g,
- fiber 2g,
- carbs 14g,
- protein 3g

Ingredients

2 tsp olive oil

3 onions, chopped finely

2 carrots, peeled and chopped finely

2 celery stick, chopped finely

3 cloves of garlic, chopped finely

250g of lean steak/beef mince

500g tomatoes pasta

1 tbsp vegetable stock

1 tsp paprika, smoked works well

4 pieces of thyme, fresh

100mg penne, wholemeal

45g parmesan cheese, grated finely

Direction

1. Take a large pan and add the oil, heat over a medium heat

2. Add the onions and cook until translucent

3. Add the carrots, garlic, and celery, cooking for 5 minutes

4. Add the mince to the pan and break it up well

5. Once the mince has browned, add the stock and the passata, adding 1 liter of hot water

6. Stir well and then add the thyme and paprika, combining once more

7. Add the lid to the pan and allow to simmer for 15 minutes

8. Add the penne and stir through, cooking for another 15 minutes

9. Add the cheese and stir

10. Serve in bowls whilst still warm.

Eggs with chilli and red Beans

Preparation time: 5 minutes

Cooking time: 5 minutes

Servings: 3

Nutrition:

- calories 550,
- fat 16g,
- fiber 32g,
- carbs18g,
- protein 43g

Ingredients

2 teaspoons of olive oil

1 red chilli, thinly sliced

1 clove of garlic, sliced

6 eggs

1 x 500g can of red beans, not drained

1 x 400 g can of tomatoes, possibly cherry tomatoes

0.25 teaspoons of cumin seeds

A little coriander, chopped

Direction

1. Take a large skillet and add the oil, letting it warm over medium-high heat
2. Add the garlic and chilli and cook until soft
3. Add the entire contents of the can of beans to the pan, along with the tomatoes, mixing thoroughly
4. Add the cumin seeds
5. Cook everything for 15 min
6. Carefully break the eggs into the pan, cook covered for 2 min
7. After a few minutes, remove the pan and add some cilantro
8. Serve still hot!

Pork Carnitas

Preparation time: 10 minutes

Cooking time: 50 minutes

Servings: 2

Nutrition:

- calories 294,
- fat 12g,
- fiber 2g,
- carbs 8g,
- protein 45g

Ingredients:

Pepper

Salt (0.25 tsp.)

Sweet and sour mushrooms (1 cup)

Dark molasses (0.5 tbsp.)

Orange juice (0.5 tbsp.)

Brown sugar (1 tbsp.)

Minced garlic clove (1 pc.)

Pork tenderloin (0.5 lb.)

Directions

1. Rinse off the pork tenderloin and blot it down with some paper towels. Slice thinly and then set it aside.

2. Place a skillet on a flame or burner set to high, and then heat it up for about a minute. Once the skillet is hot, add the pork tenderloin. Cook these for about 4 minutes until the pork is tender and cooked throughout.

3. Drain out the oil before stirring in the pepper, salt, molasses, orange juice, mushrooms and brown sugar.

4. Stir this around and simmer until your sauce is thick. Turn off the heat and let it stand for a few minutes to thicken before serving.

Turkey Walnut Salad

Preparation time: 10 min

Cooking time: 20 min

Nutrition:

- calories 390,
- fat 4g,
- fiber 2g,
- carbs 8g,
- protein 56g

Ingredients:

Chopped walnuts (0.25 cup)

Chopped celery (1 pc.)

Chopped yellow onion (0.5 pc.)

Minced turkey (8 oz.)

Pepper

Salt

1/4 cup of corn

1 cucumber cut into cubes

Parsley (2 tsp.)

Lemon juice (1 tsp.)

Dijon mustard (1 tbsp.)

Greek yogurt (2 tbsps.)

Mayo (2 tbsps.)

Dried cranberries (3 tbsps.)

Directions

1. Take out a bowl and combine the cranberries, walnuts, celery, onion, cucumber, corn and turkey.

2. In another bowl, combine the pepper, salt, parsley, lemon juice, mustard, Greek yogurt, and mayo.

3. Combine both bowls together and toss well to mix evenly before serving.

Parmesan Chicken with Zucchini

Preparation time: 10 min

Cooking time: 20 min

Servings: 6

Nutrition:

- calories 267,

- fat 34g,

- fiber 2g,

- carbs 8g,

Ingredients

Minced chicken two cups

Big zucchinis four halved along their length

Low carb tomato basil sauce

Olive oil extra virgin three tbsp.

Black olives quarter cup

Parmesan cheese quarter cup grated

Small Yellow onion diced

Mozzarella cheese quarter cup grated

Two garlic cloves minced

Basil dried one tsp.

Quarter tsp. salt

Quarter tsp. black pepper powder freshly ground

Directions

1. Heat your oven in advance at 400c.

2. Get a large pan used for baking and coat its bottom with the low carb tomato basil sauce.

3. Get a melon scooper and with care, scoop out the flesh of the zucchini. Take this flesh and blend it gently in a blender.

4. Take a large pan used for frying and add olive oil extra virgin in it. Heat the oil over medium heat and when it is hot, add in the diced yellow onion. Let the onion fry for three minutes, then add in the minced garlic and cook this for one minute until the garlic is fragrant.

5. Pour in the minced chicken and the blended flesh of zucchini. Season this with the black pepper powder freshly ground and salt. Cover and let this cook for five minutes until the chicken is well cooked. Pour out the excess fluid that may remain after the chicken is cooked.

6. Take a little of the sauce and pour it into the cooked chicken stirring so that it covers all the chicken. Let this mixture simmer over medium heat for around eight minutes.

7. Take the zucchini that has been halved and scooped and place them on a plate. Scoop the minced chicken mixture and place it in the middle of the halved zucchini. Take the stuffed zucchini pieces and place them on the dish for baking you prepared earlier.

8. Cover the dish with foil and place it in the oven you had heated in advance. Let them bake in the oven for twenty-five minutes when the zucchini softens.

9. When the zucchini is soft, take the dish for baking from the oven and unwrap the foil. Sprinkle the grated parmesan, olives, and mozzarella cheese at the top. Put back the dish for baking in the oven and let it bake until all the cheese melts well.

10. Take it from the oven and serve.

Grilled Shrimp Easy Seasoning

Preparation Time: 5 minutes

Cooking Time: 5 minutes

Servings: 4

Nutrition:

- calories 101,
- fat 3g,
- fiber 1g,
- carbs 1g,
- protein 28g

Ingredients:

Shrimp Seasoning

- 1 tsp garlic powder
- 1 tsp kosher salt
- 1 tsp Italian seasoning
- ¼ tsp cayenne pepper

Grilling

- 2 tbsps. Olive oil
- 1 tbsp. lemon juice
- 1 lb. jumbo shrimp, peeled, deveined
- Ghee for the grill

Directions:

1. Preheat the grill pan to high.
2. In a mixing bowl, stir together the seasoning ingredients.
3. Drizzle in the lemon juice and olive oil and stir.
4. Add the shrimp and toss to coat.
5. Brush the grill pan with ghee.
6. Grill the shrimp until pink, about 2-3 minutes per side.
7. Serve immediately.

The Best Garlic Cilantro Salmon

Preparation Time: 10 min

Cooking Time: 15 min

Servings: 4

Nutrition:

- calories 140,
- fat 4g,
- fiber 2g,
- carbs 3g,
- protein 20g

Ingredients:

- 1 lb. salmon filet
- 1 tbsp. butter
- 1 lemon
- 2 cups of fresh spinach leaves
- ¼ cup fresh cilantro leaves, chopped
- 4 cloves garlic, minced
- ½ tsp kosher salt
- ½ tsp freshly cracked black pepper

Directions:

1. Preheat oven to 400° F.

2. On a foil-lined baking sheet, place salmon skin side down.

3. Squeeze lemon over the salmon.

4. Season salmon with cilantro and garlic, pepper, and salt.

5. Slice butter thinly and place pieces evenly over the salmon.

6. Bake for about 7 minutes, depending on thickness.

7. Turn the oven to broil and cook 5-7 minutes, until the top is crispy.

8. Put the spinach in a glass bowl, sprinkle with half a lemon, add 2 tbsp of water, cover with cling film, put in the microwave for 2 minutes, then lay on the plate.

9. Remove the salmon from the oven and place on the spinach, serve immediately,

Cauliflower Crust Pizza

Preparation Time: 20 minutes

Cooking Time: 42 minutes

Servings: 2

Nutrition:

- Calories: 119
- Fat: 6.6 g
- Carbohydrates: 8.6 g
- Fiber: 3.4 g
- Protein: 8.3 g

Ingredients:

For Crust:

1 small head cauliflower, cut into florets

2 large organic eggs, beaten lightly

½ teaspoon dried oregano

½ teaspoon garlic powder

Ground black pepper, as required

For Topping:

½ cup sugar-free pizza sauce

¾ cup mozzarella cheese, shredded

2 tablespoons Parmesan cheese, grated

Directions:

1. Preheat your oven to F 400 (200 C).

2. Line a baking sheet with a lightly greased parchment paper.

3. Add the cauliflower in a food processor and pulse until a rice-like texture is achieved.

4. In a bowl, add the cauliflower rice, eggs, oregano, garlic powder, and black pepper and mix until well combined.

5. Place the cauliflower the mixture in the center of the prepared baking sheet and with a spatula, press into a 13-inch thin circle.

6. Bake for 40 minutes or until golden brown.

7. Remove the baking sheet from the oven. Now, set the oven to broiler on high.

8. Place the tomato sauce on top of the pizza crust and with a spatula, spread evenly, and sprinkle with the cheeses.

9. Broil for about 1-2 minutes or until the cheese is bubbly and browned.

10. Remove from oven and with a pizza cutter, cut the pizza into equal-sized triangles.

11. Serve hot.

Aromatic Dover Sole Fillets

Preparation Time: 5 minutes

Cooking Time: 20 minutes

Servings: 2

Nutrition:

- calories 244,
- fat 9g,
- fiber 2g,
- carbs 8g,
- protein 20g

Ingredients:

6 Dover Sole fillets

¼ cup virgin olive oil

The zest of 1 lemon and the juice

Dash of cardamom powder

1 cup fresh cilantro leaves

1/2 cup of Parmesan

1 cup of rocket

Pinch of sea salt

Directions:

1.Bring the fillets to room temperature.

2.Set the oven's broiler to high.

3.Pour half of the oil in an oven tray.

4.Add half of the cilantro leaves, half of the lemon zest, and the cardamom powder.

5.Lay the fillets in the mixture and top with the remaining ingredients.

6.Set under the broiler for about 7-8 minutes or until the fish breaks easily with a fork and it is not transparent.

7.Blend together the rocket, parmesan, 1 tablespoon of oil, and lemon juice. Distribute the pesto cream on fillet before serving.

8.Serve immediately.

Falafel and Tahini Sauce

Preparation Time: 10 minutes

Cooking Time: 10 minutes

Servings: 2

Nutrition:

- Calories: 281,
- Fat: 24 g
- Carbohydrates: 5 g
- Protein: 8 g

Ingredients:

½ tablespoon ground coriander

1 teaspoon kosher salt

1 tablespoon ground cumin

1 cup raw cauliflower, pureed

2 large eggs

3 tablespoons coconut flour

1 clove garlic, minced

½ teaspoon cayenne pepper

½ cup ground slivered almonds

2 tablespoons fresh parsley, chopped

Tahini sauce:

1 tablespoon lemon juice

1 clove garlic, minced

2 tablespoons tahini paste

3 tablespoons water

½ teaspoon kosher salt, more to taste if desired

Directions:

1. For the cauliflower, you should end up with a cup of the puree. It takes about 1 medium head (florets only) to get that much. First, chop it up with a knife, then add it to a food processor or magic bullet and pulse until it's blended but still has a grainy texture.

2. You can grind the almonds in a similar manner – just don't over grind them, you want the texture.

3. Combine the ground cauliflower and ground almonds in a medium bowl. Add the rest of the ingredients and stir until well blended.

4. Heat a half and half mix of olive and grape seed (or any other light oil) oil until sizzling. While it's heating, form the mix into 8 three-inch patties that are about the thickness of a hockey puck.

5. Fry them four at a time until browned on one side and then flip and cook the other side. Resist the urge to flip too soon – you should see the edges turning brown before you attempt it – maybe 4 minutes or so per side. Remove to a plate lined with a paper towel to drain any excess oil.

6. Serve with tahini sauce, and a tomato & parsley garnish if desired.

   Tahini sauce: Blend all ingredients in a bowl. Thin with more water if you like a lighter consistency.

Dinner

Spring Ramen Bowl

Preparation time: 15 min

Cooking time: 20 min

Servings: 4

Nutrition:

- calories 300,
- fat 12 g,
- fiber 1g,
- carbs 3g,
- protein 9g

Ingredients

3,5 oz. (100g) soba noodles

4 eggs

1 medium zucchini, julienned or grated

4 cups chicken stock

2 cups watercress

½ cup snap peas

1 cup mushrooms, finely sliced

1 leek (white part only), finely sliced

2 cloves garlic, minced

1 long red chili, seeded and finely chopped

1.6-inch ginger, minced

1 tsp. sesame oil

2 nori sheets, crumbled

1 lemon, cut into wedges

1 tbsp. olive oil

Directions

1. To boil the eggs, fill a saucepan with enough water to cover the eggs and set over medium heat. Bring water to a gentle boil. Add the eggs and cook for 7 minutes. Drain and transfer the eggs into cold water. Set aside.

2. Place a medium-sized saucepan over medium-low heat. Heat the olive oil and sauté the garlic, ginger, leek, and chili for 5 minutes. Add the stock, noodles, and sesame oil. Cook for another 8 minutes or until noodles are cooked according to your desired doneness. During the last minute, add the zucchini, mushroom, and watercress.

Freekeh Salad

Preparation Time: 10 minutes

Cooking Time: 10 minutes

Servings: 2

Nutrition:

- calories 800,
- fat 8g,
- fiber 2g,
- carbs 12g,
- protein 69g

Ingredients:

2 vine tomatoes, chopped or 4 cherry tomatoes, quartered

Sea salt to taste

2 tbsp olive oil

Juice of ½ lemon

Zest of ½ lemon, grated

A handful fresh cilantro or parsley, chopped

1 small cucumber, chopped

½ cup corn kernels

1 small onion, chopped

¾ cup freekeh

2 cups water

To serve:

Hummus or pesto as required

Avocado slices

Mini tortillas or wraps, as required

Direction:

1. Add freekeh and water. Place water over medium heat. When it begins to boil, lower the heat and cover with a lid. Simmer for 10-12 minutes. Uncover and cook until tender. Drain and set aside.

2. Add lemon juice, oil, zest, salt and pepper into a small bowl and whisk well.

3. Add rest of the ingredients including freekeh into a bowl and toss well. Pour dressing on top and toss well. Chill until ready to use.

4. Spread tortillas on your countertop. Place salad on one half of the tortillas. Top with avocado and hummus. Fold the other half over the filling and serve.

Garlic Shrimp with Zucchini Noodles

Preparation Time: 10 minutes

Cooking Time: 4 minutes

Servings: 3

Nutrition:

- calories 280,
- fat 8g,
- fiber 3g,
- carbs 8g,
- protein 6g

Ingredients

1 lb. shrimp, shelled and deveined

2 medium zucchinis, spiraled

2 tbsps. Fresh chives, minced

2 tbsps. Fresh lemon juice

4 garlic cloves, minced

2 tbsps. Coconut oil

Sea salt

Freshly ground black pepper

Directions

1. Place a skillet over medium heat and heat the oil.

2. Sauté the garlic about 2-3 minutes.

3. Add the shrimp and cook2-4 minutes or until pink. Remove the shrimp from the pan.

4. Add the lemon juice and stir. Bring the mixture to a boil and simmer until most of the liquid has evaporated.

5. Mix in the zucchini noodles and continue to cook another 3-4 minutes.

6. Bring the shrimp back to the skillet and season to taste. Stir well and sprinkle with chives before serving.

Veggie-stuffed Omelet

Preparation Time: 10 minutes

Cooking Time: 30 minutes

Servings: 1

Nutrition:

- calories 150,
- fat 8g,
- fiber 2g,
- carbs 8g,
- protein 24g

Ingredients

2 eggs, beaten

¼ cup mushrooms, sliced

1 cup loosely packed contemporary
   baby spinach leaves, rinsed

2 tablespoons Red bell pepper, chopped

1 tablespoon onion, chopped

1 tablespoon reduced-fat cheddar cheese, shredded

1 teaspoon olive or canola oil

1 tablespoon water

Dash salt

Dash pepper

Direction

1. Heat oil in an 8-inch nonstick skillet. Sauté the mushrooms, onion, and bell pepper for about 2 minutes until the onion is tender. Add the spinach and continue to cook, stirring

frequently, until the spinach wilts. Once cooked, transfer the vegetables to a small bowl.

2. In a medium bowl, whisk the beaten eggs, water, salt, and pepper until well combined.

3. Place the same skillet in which you cooked the vegetable mixture over medium-high heat. Add the egg mixture immediately. Make a quick, sliding back-and-forth motion with the pan, using a spatula to spread the eggs at the bottom of the pan. Once the mixture is applied, let it stand for a few seconds to brown the bottom of the omelet lightly. Do not overcook it.

4. Carefully place the vegetable mixture on the half side of the omelet. Top it with cheese and, using a spatula, gently fold the other half over the vegetables. Transfer the veggie-stuffed omelet to a plate and serve.

Picadillo Chicken

Preparation Time: 10 minutes

Cooking Time: 40 minutes

Servings: 6

Nutrition:

- calories 200,
- fat 8g,
- fiber 2g,
- carbs 8g,
- protein 24g

Ingredients:

2 tbsp oil

1 tsp ground cumin

2/3 cup chicken broth

1 pound lean ground beef

3 cup red beans, precooked

2 cup tomato sauce

Salt and pepper to taste

1/2 white onion, diced small

2 garlic cloves, minced

3 large carrots, peeled and diced small

Direction

1. In a preheated Dutch oven, add oil, onions, and garlic, and sauté until translucent.

2. Add the ground beef, carrots, and beans.

3. Pour in the tomato sauce and chicken broth. Then add the cumin, salt, and pepper; mix well.

4. Cook for 40 minutes or until the meat and carrots are cooked through and tender.

5. Delicious served on rice.

Instant Pot Teriyaki Chicken

Preparation Time: 10 minutes

Cooking Time: 20 minutes

Servings: 6

Nutrition:

- calories 200,
- fat 8g,
- fiber 2g,
- carbs 8g,
- protein 6g
- calories 200,

Ingredients:

¼ c. soy sauce or Bragg's Liquid Aminos

1 ½ tsp. ginger paste

1 c. water

1/3 c. honey

2 cloves of garlic, minced

2 pounds chicken breasts, cut into strips

2 med. green onions, sliced

3 tbsp. rice wine vinegar

For slurry:

¼ c. cold water

2 tbsp of extra virgin olive oil

3 tbsp. cornstarch

Direction

1. Heat the oil in a deep pan and fry the chicken for a few minutes.

2. Add the water, honey, soy sauce, vinegar, garlic, and ginger. Stir to incorporate, then lay the chicken breasts on top of the liquid.

3. Cook covered for 10 minutes.

4. Mix the slurry in a small bowl, making sure there are no starch lumps, then pour it over the chicken.

5. Stir the chicken to incorporate the slurry, as this will thicken the sauce. Cook for a few more minutes, occasionally stirring until the sauce has reached the desired thickness.

6. Serve over rice, salads, quinoa, or whatever you prefer!

Mixed Vegetables and Chicken Egg Rolls

Preparation Time: 10 minutes

Cooking Time: 15 minutes

Servings: 4

Nutrition:

• calories 260,

- fat 8g,
- fiber 1g,
- carbs 8g,
- protein 23g

Ingredients

1 tablespoon garlic, grated

1 tablespoon ginger, grated

4 tablespoons palm sugar, crumbled

1 banana chili, minced

4 tablespoons fish sauce

Pinch of black pepper

4 tablespoons of rice wine vinegar

1 bird eye chili, minced

8 pieces spring roll wrappers

Olive oil

Water, for sealing

1 garlic clove, minced

1 shallot, julienned

¼ cup chicken, cooked shredded

1 cup bean sprouts

1 tablespoon chicken concentrate

2 tablespoons coconut oil

¼ cup squash, julienned

¼ cup carrots, julienned

¼ cup sweet potato, julienned

¼ cup potato, julienned

½ cup of water

Pinch of sea salt

Pinch of black pepper

Direction

1. Combine dipping sauce ingredients in a bowl. Stir until sugar dissolves. Taste; adjust seasoning   if needed. Set aside.

2. To make spring rolls: pour coconut oil into large wok set over medium heat. Sauté garlic and shallot until limp and transparent; except for bean sprouts, add in remaining filling ingredients. Cook until root crops are fork tender. Toss in bean sprouts; stir. Turn off the heat immediately. Allow filling to cool completely to room temperature before rolling.

3. Add an equal portion of vegetable filling into spring roll paper; roll tightly, tucking in the edges and sealing with water. Set aside. Repeat step for remaining filling/wrapper.

4. Half-fill deep fryer with cooking oil set at medium heat; wait for the oil to become slightly rolls. Cook only until spring rolls turn golden brown, about 7 minutes.

5. Transfer cooked pieces on a plate lined with paper towels. Place 2 spring rolls on a plate; serve with dipping sauce on the side.

Cauliflower Mashed Potatoes

Preparation Time: 10 minutes

Cooking Time: 22 minutes

Servings: 3

Nutrition:

- calories 104,
- fat 8g,
- fiber 2g,
- carbs 8g,
- protein 2.5g

Ingredients

1 cup of chopped cauliflower

2 tablespoons of heavy cream

2 tablespoons of melted butter

1 tablespoon of mayonnaise

½ teaspoon of salt

Direction

1. Set your oven to 3750 F.

2. While your oven is heating up, place your 1 cup of chopped cauliflower into a heat resistant bowl followed by your 2 tablespoons of water, drizzled over the surface of the cauliflower just to make sure that maintain moisture.

3. Cook in the microwave for about 3 minutes.

4. Now take out of the microwave, deposit cauliflower into a blender, followed by your 1 tablespoon of mayonnaise, and your ½ teaspoon of salt.

5. Blend for about 1 minute before pouring the blended ingredients into your casserole dish.

6. Drizzle your 2 tablespoons of melted butter on top and stick the dish into the oven

7. Cook for 15 minutes.

8. Serve when ready.

Sheet Pan Steak Fajitas

Preparation Time: 10 minutes

Cooking Time: 25 minutes

Servings: 6

Nutrition:

- calories 450,
- fat 26g,
- fiber 2g,
- carbs 4g,
- protein 6g

Ingredients:

For the Steak:

½ jalapeño, seeded & finely diced

½ tsp. taco seasoning

1 ½ lbs. flank steak, sliced

1 lime, juiced

1 tbsp. extra virgin olive oil

1 tsp. garlic powder

Sea salt & pepper, to taste

For the Veggies:

½ tsp. taco seasoning

2 lg. onions, thinly sliced

2 tbsp. extra virgin olive oil

3 lg. bell peppers, thinly sliced

Sea salt & pepper, to taste

To Serve:

½ c. sour cream

1 sm. avocado, finely diced

2 tbsp. cilantro, fresh & finely chopped

8 oz. sharp cheddar cheese, shredded

8 small tortillas

Lime wedges

Direction

1. Preheat the oven to 475° Fahrenheit and line two large baking sheets with non-stick foil.
2. Place the meat into one large mixing bowl, and the vegetables into another.
3. In the mixing bowl with the steak, combine lime juice, taco seasoning, garlic powder, salt, and pepper. Mix completely with tongs or your hands to coat the meat completely in the juice and seasonings.
4. In the mixing bowl with the vegetables, drizzle olive oil, taco seasoning, salt, and pepper. Use hands or tongs to coat completely.
5. Pour half of each bowl onto each baking sheet, then mix thoroughly with your hands so you have two pans filled with identical mixtures.

6. Try to even out the items on the baking pan so they're in one even layer.

7. Bake for 20 minutes or until the steak has reached the desired level of doneness.

8. Broil for 5 minutes to add a little bit of crisp to the meat, then pull sheets out of the oven.

9. Season fajita mixture according to taste, if needed.

10. Serve two fajitas per person!

Coated Cauliflower Head

Preparation Time: 10 minutes

Cooking Time: 40 minutes

Servings: 6

Nutrition:

- calories 200,
- fat 8g,
- fiber 2g,
- carbs 8g,

- protein 6g

Ingredients:

2-pound cauliflower head

3 tablespoons olive oil

1 tablespoon butter, softened

1 teaspoon ground coriander

1 teaspoon salt

1 egg, whisked

1 teaspoon dried cilantro

1 teaspoon dried oregano

1 teaspoon tahini paste

Directions:

1. Trim cauliflower head if needed.

2. Preheat oven to 350F.

3. In the mixing bowl, mix up together olive oil, softened butter, ground coriander, salt, whisked egg, dried cilantro, dried oregano, and tahini paste.

4. Then brush the cauliflower head with this mixture generously and transfer in the tray.

5. Bake the cauliflower head for 40 minutes.

6. Brush it with the remaining oil mixture every 10 minutes.

Snacks for Tasting

Roasted Brussels sprouts With Mushrooms

Preparation Time: 10 minutes

Cooking Time: 35 minutes

Servings: 4

Nutrition:

- Calories: 149,
- Fat: 11 g
- Carbohydrates: 10 g
- Fiber: 4 g
- Protein: 5 g

Ingredients:

Brussels Sprouts, fresh - 1 pound

Mushrooms, chopped - 1 cup

Olive oil - 1 tablespoon

Extra olive oil to oil the baking tray

Pepper and salt for tasting

Gorgonzola cheese - ¼ cup

(If you prefer not to use the Gorgonzola cheese,

you can toss the Brussels sprouts when hot,

with 2 tablespoons of butter instead.

Directions:

1.Warm the oven to 350 degrees Fahrenheit or 175 Celsius.

2.Rub a large pan or any vessel you wish to use with a little bit of olive oil. You can use a paper towel or a pastry brush.

3.Cut off the ends of the Brussels sprouts if you need to and then cut then in a lengthwise direction into halves. (Fear not if a few of the leaves come off of them, some may become deliciously crunchy during cooking)

4.Cut the mushrooms.

5.Put your Brussels sprouts as well as the sliced mushrooms inside a bowl, and cover them all with some olive oil, pepper, and salt (be generous).

6.Arrange all of your mushrooms and Brussels sprouts onto your roasting pan in a single layer.

7.Roast this for 30 to 35 minutes, or when they become tender and can be pierced with a fork easily. Stir during cooking if you wish to get a more even browning.

8.Once cooked, toss them with the Gorgonzola Cheese (or butter) before you serve them. Serve them hot.

Eggplant Fries

Preparation Time: 10 minutes
Cooking Time: 15 minutes
Servings: 8
Nutrition
- Calories: 212,
- Fat: 15.8 g
- Carbohydrates: 12.1 g
- Protein: 8.6 g

Ingredients:

2 eggs

2 cups almond flour

2 tablespoons coconut oil, spray

2 eggplant, peeled and cut thinly

Salt and pepper

Directions:

1. Preheat your oven to 400 degrees Fahrenheit

2. Take a bowl and mix with salt and black pepper in it

3. Take another bowl and beat eggs until frothy

4. Dip the eggplant pieces into eggs

5. Then coat them with flour mixture

6. Add another layer of flour and egg

7. Then, take a baking sheet and grease with coconut oil on top

8. Bake for about 15 minutes

9. Serve and enjoy.

Parmesan Crisps

Preparation Time: 5 minutes

Cooking Time: 25 minutes

Servings: 8

Nutrition:

- Calories: 133,
- Fat: 11 g
- Carbohydrates: 1g
- Protein: 11 g

Ingredients:

1 teaspoon butter

8 ounces parmesan cheese,

full fat and shredded

Directions:

1. Preheat your oven to 400 degrees F
2. Put parchment paper on a baking sheet and grease with butter
3. Spoon parmesan into 8 mounds, spreading them apart evenly
4. Flatten them
5. Bake for 5 minutes until browned
6. Let them cool
7. Serve and enjoy.

Roasted Broccoli

Preparation Time: 5 minutes

Cooking Time: 20 minutes

Servings: 4

Nutrition:

- Calories: 62,
- Fat: 4 g
- Carbohydrates: 4 g
- Protein: 4 g

Ingredients:

4 cups broccoli florets

1 tablespoon olive oil

Salt and pepper to taste

Directions:

1. Preheat your oven to 400 degrees F
2. Add broccoli in a zip bag alongside oil and shake until coated
3. Add seasoning and shake again
4. Spread broccoli out on the baking sheet, bake for 20 minutes
5. Let it cool and serve.

Healthy Salmon Sandwich

Preparation Time: 10 minutes

Cooking Time: 10 minutes

Servings: 6

Nutrition:

- Calories 280
- Fats 20g
- Protein 15g
- Carbohydrates 12g

Ingredients

2 salmon fillets (1 Lb)

12 slices of vegan bread

2 eggs

1/2 cup chopped onions

1 tbsp mayonnaise

1 cup gluten-free bread crumbs

2 tsp lemon juice

1/4 tsp garlic salt

1 tbsp chopped fresh parsley

2 tbsp olive oil

Directions

1. Season the salmon using salt and pepper.

2. In a skillet add ½ tbsp of oil and heat it over medium heat.

3. Fry the salmon for 2 minutes on both sides.

4. Let it cool down completely.

5. Remove them bones and mash it finely.

6. In a bowl transfer the salmon. Add the onion, garlic salt, parsley, bread crumbs, mayo and eggs.

7. Pull well with the fork.

8. Let it refrigerate for 30 minutes.

9. In a skillet heat the remaining oil.

10. Fry the slices of bread on both sides.

11. Make sure to fry in batches.

12. Assemble the salad sandwich to taste. Serve hot.

Santorini Bay Salad

Preparation Time: 10 minutes

Cooking Time: 15 minutes

Servings: 4

Nutrition:

- Calories 360

- Carbohydrates 32g

- Fat 23g

- Protein 12g

Ingredients:

¼ cup of red onion, finely chopped

½ cup of feta cheese crumbles

½ cup of finely chopped parsley

½ cucumber, chopped

1 cup of quinoa, cooked and cooled

1 cup of cooked chickpeas

1 lemon

1 pepper, chopped

10 cherry tomatoes, cut in half

1 tablespoon. cumin

2 tbsp. extra virgin olive oil

20 pitted black olives

Sea salt and pepper, just enough

Directions:

1. In a medium bowl, mix all ingredients thoroughly.

2. Cover and refrigerate for 15 minutes before serving.

Baked Fennel

Preparation Time: 10 minutes;

Cooking Time: 50 minutes;

Servings: 6

Nutrition:

Calories: 75,

Fat: 2g,

Protein: 3g,

Carbs: 12g

Ingredients:

Fennel bulbs - 3

Chicken broth - 1 cup

Gorgonzola cheese, crumbled - ¼ cup

Panko bread crumbs - ¼ cup

Salt

Pepper

Directions:

1.Cut the fennel bulbs in half lengthwise through the root end.

2.Put the fennel cut-side down in a skillet and add the chicken broth. Cover and simmer for 20 minutes.

3.Preheat oven to 375°F. Place cooked fennel bulbs in a baking dish, cut-sides up.

4.Mix the Gorgonzola with the bread crumbs and divide the mixture evenly on the top of each fennel bulb.

5.Bake for 25 minutes, season with salt and pepper and serve hot.

Summer Swiss Chard

Preparation Time: 5 minutes;

Cooking Time: 15 minutes;

Servings: 4

Nutrition:

- Calories: 132,
- Fat: 11g,
- Protein: 3g,
- Carbs: 8g

Ingredients:

Swiss chard - 1 pound.

Olive oil - 3 tablespoons.

Onion, diced - 1 cup.

Salt

Orange 1 piece

Oregano - ½ teaspoon.

Red-wine vinegar - 3 tablespoons.

Salt

Pepper

Directions:

1. Chop the chard and set aside.

2. Heat the olive oil in a skillet over medium heat.

3. Add the diced onion, a pinch of salt, and oregano and cook until the onions are tender.

4. Add the chopped chard, chopped orange and sauté for a few minutes and then remove from heat.

5. Stir in the vinegar and season with salt and pepper.

Tofu and Broccoli Salad

Preparation Time: 10 minutes;

Cooking Time: 10 minutes;

Servings: 4

Nutrition:

- Calories: 95,

- Fat: 6g,

- Protein: 8g,

- Carbs: 16g

Ingredients:

1 lb tofu, cubed

1 onion, sliced

1 cup broccoli, divided into florets

2 red bell peppers, sliced

2 tablespoons olive oil

1 tablespoon sesame oil

1 garlic clove, crushed

1 carrot, julienne strips

1 stick celery, sliced

1 tablespoon tamarind concentrate

1 tablespoon tomato puree

2 tablespoons oyster sauce

1 tablespoon light soy sauce

1 tablespoon chilli sauce

1 tablespoon fish sauce

Pinch of ground star anise

8 oz mangetout snow peas, halved

4 oz thin French beans, halved

2 tablespoons sugar

1 teaspoon cornflour

2 cups water

1 tablespoon white wine vinegar

Directions:

1.In a wok, heat the oil. Add garlic and cook for 2 minutes.

2.Add tofu in batches or until golden brown on all sides. Remove and set aside.

3.Add onion, red bell pepper, celery, carrots, snow peas, green beans, and broccoli for 3 minutes or until tender crisp.

4.Add oyster sauce, fish sauce, chilli sauce, vinegar, tomato puree, sugar, and star anise in a bowl. Mix well.

5.Mix the cornflour with water. Add to the tofu. Stir fry until the sauce boils and thickens. Serve.

Desserts

Soles Banana Cupcakes

Preparation Time:10 minutes

Cooking Time:20 minutes

Servings:4

Nutrition:

Calories: 142

Fat: 5.8 g

Fiber: 4.2 g

Carbs: 5.7 g

Protein: 1.6 g

Ingredients:

Four tablespoons avocado oil

Four eggs

½ cup of orange juice

Two teaspoons cinnamon powder

One teaspoon vanilla extract

Two bananas, peeled and chopped

¾ cup almond flour

½ teaspoon baking powder

Cooking spray

Directions:

1. In a bowl, combine the oil with the eggs, orange juice, and the other ingredients except for the cooking spray. Whisk well, pour in a cupcake pan greased with the cooking spray, and introduce it in the oven 350 degrees F bake for 20 minutes.

2. Cool the cupcakes down and serve.

Almond Rice Dessert

Preparation Time:10 minutes

Cooking Time:20 minutes

Servings:4

Nutrition:

• Calories: 234

- Fat: 9.5 g
- Fiber: 3.4 g
- Carbs: 12.4 g
- Protein: 6.5 g

Ingredients:

1 cup white rice

2 cups almond milk

1 cup almonds, chopped

½ cup stevia

One tablespoon cinnamon powder

½ cup pomegranate seeds

Directions:

1. In a pot, blend the rice with the milk and stevia, bring it to a simmer and cook for 20 minutes, stirring often.

2. Add the rest of the ingredients, stir, divide into bowls, and serve.

Mango Cream

Preparation Time: 30 minutes

Cooking Time: 0 minutes

Servings: 4

Nutrition:

Calories: 132

Fat: 4 g

Fiber: 6.3 g

Carbs: 6.8 g

Protein: 4.8 g

Ingredients:

3 cups mango, cut into medium chunks

½ cup of coconut water

¼ cup stevia

1 teaspoon vanilla extract

Directions:

1. Mix the mango with the rest of the ingredients in a blender. Pulse well, divide into bowls, and serve cold.

Chocolate Mousse

Preparation time: 5 minutes

Cooking time: 40 minutes

Servings: 6

Nutrition:

- Calories 166
- Protein 9g
- Carbohydrates 2.4g
- Fat 13.5g
- Fiber 0.3g

Ingredients:

Cocoa powder – .33 cup

Lakanto monk fruit sweetener – 2 tablespoons

Heavy whipping cream – 1.5 cups

Directions:

1.Place the heavy cream in a bowl and use a hand mixer or stand mixer to beat it on medium speed.

2.Once the cream begins to thicken, add the monk fruit sweetener and cocoa and continue to beat it until stiff peaks form.

3.Serve the mousse immediately or store it in the fridge for up to twenty-four hours before enjoying it. If desired, you can serve it with Lily's stevia-sweetened chocolate for chunks.

Berries with Ricotta Cream

Preparation time: 5 min

Cooking time: 40 min

Servings: 6

Nutrition:

- Calories 153
- Protein 6.2g
- Carbohydrates 19.2g

- Fat 5.6g
- Fiber 2.6g

Ingredients:

Ricotta, whole milk – 1.5 cups

Heavy cream – 2 tablespoons

Lemon zest – 1.5 teaspoons

Swerve confectioner's sweetener – .25 cup

Vanilla extract – 1 teaspoon

Blackberries - .5 cup

Raspberries - .5 cup

Blueberries - .5 cup

Directions:

1.In a large bowl, add all of the ingredients, except for the berries, and whip them together with a hand mixer until completely smooth.

2.Set out four parfait glasses and divide half of the berries between all of them. Top the berries with half of the ricotta mixture, the remaining half of the berries, and lastly, the second half of the ricotta mixture.

3.Serve the parfaits immediately or within the next twenty-four hours.

Easy Chocolate Pudding

Preparation time: 5 minutes

Cooking time: 30 minutes

Servings: 6

Nutrition:

- Calories 231
- Protein 14.9g
- Carbohydrates 3.2g
- Fat 18g
- Fiber 1.1g

Ingredients:

1 ½ cups organic coconut cream from a can

½ cup raw cacao powder

(sifted unsweetened cocoa powder works as well)

6 tablespoons pure maple syrup (may adjust to up

to 8 tablespoons, depending on how sweet you like it)

2 teaspoons pure vanilla extract

Fine-grain sea salt

Directions:

1.In a small saucepan over low heat, whisk coconut cream, cacao, and maple syrup until smooth. A smaller whisk my make a smoother mixture. Continue to cook over low/medium for 2 minutes, or until the mixture just starts to come to a boil with small bubbles.

2.Remove from heat. Add salt and vanilla. Stir. Taste and add more maple if you'd like a sweeter pudding.

3.Pour into individual containers/bowls or keep in one larger bowl to set.

4.Cover and refrigerate until set, or overnight for a thick and creamy pudding. Makes 4 servings.

Almond Bites

Preparation Time: 10 Minutes

Cooking Time: 14 Minutes

Servings: 5

Nutrition:

- Calories: 118,
- Fats: 11.5 g,
- Carbohydrates: 2.4 g,
- Protein: 2.7 g

Ingredients:

1 cup almond flour

¼ cup almond milk

1 egg; whisked

2 tbsp. butter

1 tbsp. coconut flakes

½ tsp. baking powder

½ tsp. apple cider vinegar

½ tsp. vanilla extract

Directions:

1.Mix up together the whisked egg, almond milk, apple cider vinegar, baking powder, vanilla extract, and butter

2.Stir the mixture and add almond flour and coconut flakes. Knead the dough.

3.If the dough is sticky, add more almond flour. Make medium balls from the dough and place them on the wire rack on a lined baking sheet.

4.Bake the cake in the preheated oven for 12 minutes at 360 degrees F.

5.Check if the dessert is cooked; and cook for 2 minutes more for a crunchy crust

Coconut Macaroon Cookies

Preparation Time: 5 Minutes

Cooking Time: 15 Minutes

Servings: 18

Nutrition:

- Calories: 150,

- Fat: 7 g,

- Carbohydrates: 20 g,

- Protein 2 g

Ingredients:

5 cups coconut (finely shredded, unsweetened)

1 1/2 cup brown sugar

Pinch of salt

4 large egg whites (lightly beaten)

1 teaspoon pure vanilla extract

Directions:

1. Preheat the oven to 350 F. Line 2 large baking sheets with parchment paper.

2. In a large mixing bowl, mix the coconut, sugar, and salt. Add the egg whites and vanilla extract, mixing until well combined.

3. Using your hands, form the mixture into small 1 1/2 to 2 tablespoon mounds, transferring each to the prepared baking sheets as you work.

4. Bake until just the cookies' peaks is light golden brown, about 12 to 15 minutes, turning the pan halfway through to ensure even baking.

5. Allow the cookies to cool completely on a wire cooling rack. Serve at room temperature.

Coconut Protein Balls

Preparation Time: 20 minutes

Cooking Time: 0 minutes

Servings: 27

Nutrition

- Calories 108
- Carbohydrates 16g
- Fats 4g
- Protein 5g

Ingredients:

¼ cup dark chocolate chips

½ cup coconut flakes, unsweetened

½ cup water

1 ½ cup almonds, raw & unsalted

2 tbsp. cocoa powder, unsweetened

3 cup Medjool dates, pitted

4 scoops whey protein powder, unsweetened

Directions:

1.Blend almonds in a food processor until a flour is formed. Add the water and dates to the flour and continue to process until thoroughly combined. You may need to stop intermittently to scrape down the sides of the bowl.

2.Add cocoa and protein to the processor and continue to process until well combined. You may need to stop intermittently to scrape down the sides of the bowl.

3.Pull the blade out of the processor (carefully!) and use your spatula to gather all of the dough in one place inside the processor container.

4.On a plate or in a large, shallow dish, spread the coconut flakes.

5.Scoop out a little bit of the dough at a time using a spoon, and roll it into balls, then move each one in the coconut flakes.

6.Refrigerate for at least 30 min before enjoying.

Vegan Coconut Kefir Banana Muffins

Preparation Time: 5 minutes

Cooking Time: 60 minutes

Servings: 6

Nutrition:

- calories 212,
- fat 7g,
- fiber 2g,
- carbs 35g,
- protein 2g

Ingredients

All-purpose flour, one and a half cups

Crushed sugar, 1 cup

Unsweetened shredded coconut 250 mL

Baking soda 2 teaspoon

Baking powder 1 teaspoon

Salt 1/2 tsp

Ripe mashed bananas 2

Coconut milk, dairy-free one and a half cups

Pure Vanilla extract 1 tsp

Liquid Coconut Oil, - 1/4cup

Direction

1. Settle the oven to 180° C. Sprinkle cooking spray on muffin tin. Put it aside.

2. In a big bowl, whisk together sugar, flour, baking powder, shredded coconut, salt, and baking soda. Place it aside.

3. In a separate big cup, mix bananas, vanilla, and coconut oil. Put the flour and mix, whisk until there are no white stripes left.

4. Add mixture in muffin pot. Keep baking till the upper parts are golden and the spatula put in the middle comes out clear, around 30 minutes. Allow chilling the muffin tin for 15 minutes.

Conclusion

Regardless of the ease of an intermittent fast, it can still be one of the most difficult things you ever do if you have never fasted before. You need to regulate your diet cycle, which can be quite a task for many. Yet, it can't be compared to the grueling fact that you need to go 'hungry' for 8-10-12 or even more hours of the day. Eating one or two meals per day and going 'hungry' for the rest is especially difficult for people who are busy and are often accustomed to eating anything they find whenever they get the time. Such people avoid doing intermittent fasting because they believe that they cannot stick to the diet or will go hungry.

Since intermittent fasting is not limiting in what you can eat, there is a wide variety to choose from. All you should have in mind is the number of calories you are consuming per meal. Meals that have low carbohydrate content are ideal because they, in turn, have low caloric content as well. Having more lean meats, fruits, and vegetables is ideal together with grains too.

Intermittent fasting isn't only an approach to shied weight; however, it is an approach to transform you completely, and in doing-as such, dragging out it. The medical advantages are perpetual, particularly when they are joined with work out, making this nourishment experience something unquestionably worth investigating. The primary concern is — the individuals who are on this eating regimen have lower death rates than the individuals who are not, which is reason enough to try it out. In the event that you have a past filled

94

with coronary illness in your family, you truly can't stand to proceed in a similar way, and now you have another option.

CPSIA information can be obtained
at www.ICGtesting.com
Printed in the USA
BVHW092103250621
610374BV00006B/992